Tonight

Tonight

Poetry by

Natalie J. Case

Contents

Dedication

Words decorate my life. Music fills my soul.

Where words and music marry, I find solace.

So I dedicate this collection of poetry to the songwriters, the poets, and the musicians.

You make my life a beautiful place to live.

An Introduction

Sometimes my head spins with words and they tumble out of my fingers and onto the page where I can poke at them until they end up in a pleasing configuration.

My poetry has always tended toward the darker emotions, commentary on society, and adult relationships. That's what you will find here. Some of it rhymes, most of it doesn't. Some deal with alcohol and sex. Others are angry and raw. And there are a few that are just silly or that don't have a deep meaning, I just liked the way they sound.

I was going to put them all into some order, categorized neatly into boxes where the poems all relate, but poetry is messy, raw, so I decided to just throw them all together in a way that I thought worked for me.

I invite you to come wander through the magic of words with me.

I'm Not Myself Tonight

I got drunk again tonight
    and you know I don't drink
thinking about you, and the bad times
    together don't we make an art out of war?
and the way your tongue had
of finding that spot
    no one else can do it like you
I downed four rum-n-cokes in an hour's time
fucking myself furiously against the pain
    like you used to
smoking half a pack of Marlboro lights
    and I haven't smoked in years
as I watched some stupid old movie
with Ingrid Bergman in tears
    I wish I could cry like that
    without smudging my face
I keep thinking I should stop thinking
your face, your hands... your tongue
    but we both know you're a part of me
my callous heart turns away from you
    like some orgasmic nightmare
I should forget you
    stop touching myself
and this bottle of Bacardi Gold taunting me
    dare me to walk away
to succumb to your scandal, your seduction
    forgive me if I do
    I'm not myself tonight

2 am

I worried that I wasn't good enough
that my mistakes
were the cause
of your failure

I knew that I was crazy
a little girl lost
inside the raving lunacy
of adolescence

I thought I could
fix it all
by fixing myself
quieting the voices
that called me
out to dance on the lawn
at 2 am

I only discovered
that I wasn't broken
just mislead
and the truth is
I like dancing
on cold grass
to the music of the stars

Talk Dirty to Me

I promised myself wine and roses tonight
but gave in to Bacardi instead
  not that I'm drunk
feeling more like Stallone
than Gere
  I'm not picky
  I just know what I want
frustration penetrates my desire
  just like you do me
have you ever wanted
to crawl out of your skin
  let me borrow yours
  I want to crawl inside you
and bask naked in the sun
  hot, like your breath
  on my navel
dance for me
stripping thoughts
and masks
  you know I melt
  when you talk dirty to me
all the unnecessary bullshit
  like so much
  dirty laundry
moving fluidly
primordially
  is this what gods feel
   when they touch?

4

Evening Star

shine upon me, evening star
awaken within me
that which I've lost, sacrificed
in the name of purity
on the cold marble
altars of man
remember me
daughter of your daughter
forgotten in this modern wasteland
of sexual suppression, unnatural order
my loins grow weak, wet
as the fire kindles, slowly,
Astarte, Goddess, Warrior
Lover of sensuality
sexuality
free me of their guilt
slide open my legs to know
passion's kiss, pleasure's sweet caress
guide this body toward ecstasy
given to bring love and lust
together in one moment
of climactic thunder
exploding into the night sky
where you shine
your light, calling me
to shed the chains of my
sexual slavery

falling away

I waited for you in the dark tonight
my cheeks stained with memory
the taste of bile sharp in a mouth lined with lies
bitter and shrill
the bite of emptiness
hollow echoes haunting
hallways littered with nothing
brittle air
hot and thin and already breaking open
kissing lips laced with dust
falling away
from
you

Sibyl of Cumae

eternity wrested from the gods
in a promise never kept
    would it have been so bad
        to have a god as your lover?
bought with seduction
sweetly plied
    though your heart was never in it
oracle of Apollo's light
whispering hidden truths
in disfigured phrases
    even then you knew the truth, didn't you?
wasting into the Womb of Life
selling wisdom
to kings
    you were a goddess even then you know
in enigmatic pages
scribbled delusions
of inspirational madness
    or did you just make it seem that way?
foretelling distant moments

and dreams to come
on leaves that the wind carried away
      I'll bet you planned it that way...
      watching from the darkness of your cave
while eternity conspired
against you
      what was it that made you change your mind?
withering the frailty
of your human body,
your mortal soul
      did you cry out for mercy
      in those moments you were sane?
until even you,
once proud enough
to claim Apollo as your lover
      though you never did...I can't imagine why
would beg any who could hear you
      can the children in Naples still hear your voice?
for the release
of death

Trespass Slowly

the glow of wine warms me
a bottle and a half
of Merlot
my skin burns as our words
turn to forbidden thoughts
a friend,
a warm desire
your touch traces fire
across my cheek
leaving me parched
and gasping for air
our lips
trespass slowly
upon flesh left bare
never reaching

for what we both desire most
        your mouth
                forms a perfect seal
        moist and hot
                around my breast
my lips part to yours
and the pleasure
of that kiss
ripples through my body
        how long have we waited
        to taste this
taboos broken
we grasp at each other
like desperate lovers
after a decade apart
        breathlessly caressing
        our deepest intimacies
the way our words always have

collecting myself

pieces of who I am
who I thought I was
scattered across
a lifetime of moments
scribbled in crayon on dinner napkins
like the phone number
of a one night stand
forgotten the next day
lost in muttered phrases
repeating unending in the corners of my brain
tossed around with
all the pieces of those
I have passed along the way
in some lucid daydream
of wildflowers with faces
that I pick and choose
collecting myself together again
in the basket of my soul
reclaiming the pieces
of who I am

rebirth

kneeling in obscurity, beneath my own desires
buried by the residue of someone else's pyre
hidden in the memory of long forgotten dreams
scattered and divided and torn up at the seams
trapped within the passions that I must never show
holding to the fantasies that I might never know
severed from the things I want by those who care for me
clinging to my prison walls and praying to be free
clutched inside another's pain, held fast within the fears
drowning in an ocean of dry and unshed tears
longing for the freedom that fills my dreams each night
to cast aside this cloak of doubt and climb into the light
knowing if I do not try, then I will never know,
anxiously awaiting, alone, afraid to go
scattered, yet repairing, mending up the seams
finding an increasing strength in my old and tattered dreams
kneeling in obscurity, holding my desire
building in the ruins a small, but growing, fire

Guilt

I ply my conscience
with alcohol
afraid to let the truth run rampant
afraid
the truth may yet set me
free
guilt
is a wasted emotion
felt only by those with no need
of guilt
and lost
on sinners like me
with their inconsolable needs
and the promise of another drink
our solitude held
sacrosanct
even in the privacy
of a pew

The Forgotten Wait Alone

dogma in deafening decibels
screaming struggles for our souls
secular semantics
filling hollow, empty holes
forgotten faith and freedom
a destiny designed
a world where will and wonder
are quickly undermined
gods of glitter and gaiety
adorn administrative walls
and devils dressed in papal robes
hold hell in hallowed halls
reverence raped and ravaged
privileged power now presides
in the courts of human worship
while a world at war takes sides
and somewhere far beneath it all
in anguish all their own
in blind and brooding silence
the forgotten wait alone

Odin

Odin, father of heroes and gods
     All-Father, do you watch me now?
I can feel your blood inside my veins
burning into me
     spilling red across my brain
like blood on snow
battle-field carnage unending
claiming souls for the magic feast
     a poet seeking wisdom in the entrails and blood
the Valkyries' song frightening and true
     gathering warriors to Valhalla
     where you treat them to feasting and war
honorable duty paid with an eternity
of food and fighting
     do your loins tremble
     when Freya chooses her slain
     leaving you to watch silently?
or does your heart skip to know
that your people have been scattered?
     do you ever tire of the blood?
or is that what made you
hang yourself from the tree
     in the center of the Worlds
upside down
     sacrificing yourself for wisdom
what fantasies did you dream there?
did you see it all, the final ending
     was it bloody enough to satisfy you?

Red

pins
and needles
piercing
flesh and crust
barbed words
punch through
tearing at
the tender
crust
of
the scab
that isn't
thick enough
to deny
the penetration

sticky heat
pools
cools
rests within
never forgotten
a stain
that colors
my view
of the world red
smeared and scattered
with hate

The Morrigan

celtic crow, bane of inconsistent souls
vainly inviting the pleasure of the Morrigan
daring for the maiden's choice to Divine Right
diadems of gold gifted with her maidenhead
offered in return for warming her cold heart
with pleasures given in marriage beds to queens
consummating mortal crowns with immortality

carnal desires give birth to carnal seeds
all mortal men fall guilty, greedy
craving beyond her gift, so warmly given
mother of the modern bitch,
so desired and feared the same
Queen Maeve, with panic's passion
clad in Nemain's awesome cloak
shifts from maiden to raven in fury
wading through the gore of battle
in black leather and crow feather
with a taste for destruction's bile

shiver of death rightly earned
at the hands of the Warrior Queen
in retrospect he knows his sin
and welcomes his reward
the crone's favor is withdrawn
for mortal vanity begun
in the preconception of her gift

I feel like wearing war paint

today I feel like wearing war paint
across my face
and tying an eagle feather
into my hair
I feel like putting on deerskin
and crying out a fearsome
battle cry

today I feel like seeing the sun
upon my skin
and hearing the wind sing
around me
I feel like dancing the dance
of war around the fire
and raising my spear to the heavens
to pray for victory

but today the red has drained
from my skin
and it is softened by the white light
of fluorescent bulbs

I wear high heels and stockings
of nylon,
the color of my grandfather's skin
to hide me

and today my war paint has been muted
into acceptable shades
for the white skin which colors me
and dark hair has been bound into corporate style
lightened by chemicals and untouched by the wind

today I feel like wearing war paint
across my face
and letting my hair fly free
dancing with the wind
as long lost friends
I feel like praying to the Great Spirit
with my face turned
toward the Sun
becoming one with the Ancestors
my heart at peace
within me

Consuming Gods

the ancient evils have left this earth
and the Great Gods have gone away
the remnant of half-remembered beliefs
shade the truths to appear absolute,
relevant to what we see in distant specters
of our past and future gathering to mock us
and in all our impudent knowledge,
our horrendous, horrific heresy,
we search for deep, meaningful answers,
thundering monumental prayers at heaven
as if our words can rouse the Gods from their slumber
all comatose, captive, broken upon the altars
of common human disbelief and apathy
their own creation consuming their existence
to feed themselves

Almost Love

How long have we been together now
since that day in the snow
When you took my hand to warm it
since we held hands at that show
You kissed me in the spring
outside the college dorms
We made love in the summer, to the sound of thunderstorms

We came together seamlessly
a nearly perfect fit
I bought a ring, I made a vow
I thought that this was it
Your smile still makes me happy
but the spark just isn't there
Like trying to catch a firefly, and getting only air

We move through the motions
holding hands, making love
We dance against the current
we pull, we shove
It's warm and it's safe
but isn't what I'm dreaming of
And I think maybe the hardest part Is that it was almost love

death dream

the earth is cold tonight
leaching heat
from my skin
    my bones
quiet and alone
    you left me here
the sky is dark
walls of dirt
embrace me
    my only solace
sleep lingers
heavy on my face
    sleep, my love
did I dream
your face
above my grave
    did you come for me
or is this grave
the dream

Wild Hunt

there was a time when I was meek
but I haven't been that way in years
Merlin's soul kissed me
as I wandered the foreign woods
in the womb of my Mother, in the arms of my Father
Great God of the Wild Hunt
I fell in love
I became this woman, this huntress
the taste of blood
becomes me
Oh Horned God, who taught me the value
of my own life
Cernunnos, lover of my inhibitions
ride with me
across the night skies
taste the thrill of the hunt
stand still the hearts of mortal men
to see the terrible
beauty of what you have made in me
no longer meek
no longer soft
this huntress
with the taste for blood,
vengeance
Father, transform me
into this wild creature
let me run beside you
in the hunt

infinity forgives

infinity forgives
the harshness of the moment
the careless taking
the emotional response
she sees
humanity trapped
within our finite paths
temporal beings
traveling eternal crossroads
following weary footsteps
from the dust of Dawn
to the dust of Death
she offers freedom
beyond morality
in the cradle of her arms
her hushed voice
soothing and restful
whispering peace

jagged

I am not easy to love tonight
    my curves turn sharp,
        my song a razor
you don't want to get too close
the wheels are spinning tonight
    if you catch me
        you might bleed
the scars crack open
heat seeps skin to skin
jagged edges rip
    don't touch me now
        don't touch me there
pain in silence screeches
whistles against broken edges
howls out
of deserted walls and windows
    I'm not home
        I'm not there
there is no home tonight
there is no safe place
    smoke obscures the danger
        I can't breathe
            can't breathe
put away your nice words
your platitudes
your attitudes
    judge me
        hate me
            fuck you

crescendo

I fell asleep alone tonight
but for the bottle of booze
    liquid fire burning inside me
        the way you used to
and I dreamed of lips and hands
touching me
    dirty fingers playing
        on the strings
            crescendo, crescendo
riding for the finish line
faster
    harder
deeper
    more
until the drums break open
    molten ecstasy
        pours
and the thundering pace
falls silent
    gasping as the river freezes
winter comes early
when the sun sets low
    tomorrow I'll be strong
        tonight I just need the heat
burning distant and cold

come inside

I felt your head
in my hands tonight
    it made me want you
drowsy and sated
still warm
from the afternoon sun
    your skin glows
        I crave the taste of you
your sighs quake
my body
as I lay you down
    your sweat
    is sweet
your brow glistens
your eyes
penetrate me
    come inside
    I need you

promises

it feels like tomorrow tonight
    fresh promises
clean, like morning air
    I ache
        holding you
your face streaked
with the agony
of admitting it all
    pressing into
    my emotional debris
and somewhere between
    our last fuck
        and your first tear
something changed
    in me, in you
no going back
    now that the words
        have been spoken

beat up

I am beat up tonight
tired in my bones
and you show up
> *in your cowboy boots*
>> *like the rodeo's in town*

wanting
needing this thing
we have between us
> *my body aches*

this sweat drenched rodeo
all our own
> *you make me feel*
> *tired*

like I've been *breaking bucks*
> *my whole life*

can't we just rest a while
> *I only ride the wild ones*
> *don't I?*

can't we just
be friends again
> *we both know*
> *I'll let you in*

ride for tomorrow
> *I'm closer to oblivion*
> *when you're inside me*

blues tonight

it's a blues kind of night tonight
guitar
singing
    moaning
warm red wine
stains my lips
as I watch you sleep
    I never knew
    you could look
      so soft
        so lovely
we laughed tonight
better than old times
    the wine
    seduced us
your kiss was chaste
    an apology
offered promises
    forgiveness
an invitation
    an offering
    to bliss

Alone

I walked alone tonight
the sound of my steps distant
in my ears
as I put my feet
to the cold ground
no soul but mine
out there
under starless skies
no one to see me

Desire

skin whispers over skin
following the curve
of hip and thigh
warm from the sun
lips murmur over lips
sharing breath
taste
desire
heat pools
between
and we
are
one

Death's Angel Fair

pause here, I pray thee, while making your rounds
of the disheveled, disheartened and desolate bound
forgive for the moment, this intrusion too dear
and lay soft thy hand on the misery here
oh, angel of endings, bring thy kiss so sweet
to ease them their burdens and raise them complete
touch wounded souls, lost in despair
the promise of freedom from death's angel fair
relief in this moment, a lifetime of pain
joy now restored in sweet, sad refrain
promise me, angel, when my time has come
your touch will be gentle as you carry me home

Fire and Ice

there is ice in my veins tonight
weakening the fire
in my heart
and I crave
the taste of smoke
on my tongue
the flush of heat
in my skin
the callous burn
of the flame

friends

my friends are electronic
I see them in a box
defined by tiny pixels
pictures made of blocks
I see them every day
from the safety of my house
I speak to them through keyboards
and the clicky-click of a mouse
some I've known for decades
and some I've never met
some I take for granted
and some I can't forget
we share our lives in moments
mundane and morose
in cats and dogs and kids
and memes a daily dose
through a year of hell on earth
with traffic quite contained
it was my electronic friends
that kept me entertained

Atlanta

I believe it must be raining in Atlanta
but there's no control for that
the washing of a soul requires
some response from me
but I make no claim to the answers
which you seek
the dreams with which I understand
enlighten none but me
and the truths which I speak are my own
in mythical proportions I am nothing
yet I am
and I believe it must be raining in Atlanta
the tears are not my own
and there is no control for that

Climax

I come before you
wearing my anticipation
and little else
apprehension
and ecstasy
mingle in sweat
with passionate forays
into intimate places
daring the senses
to comprehend
the shivering
orgasm
climax screaming
as bodies collide
steam rises
from heated flesh
and disappears
in the night

Two Souls Departing

Beauty, he says
    Beauty, she sighs wearily
looking together on the site
    where once they were
Peace, he murmurs
    And Pain, she breathes
raining tears on those
    who watch from below
    without seeing

an angel

a moment ago an angel,
glimpsed at the corners of perception,
standing alone in the unpeopled space
of my blind eyes' reception
turned to me a tranquil face,
and my soul, at once serene,
lifted up its weary head
and let go of haggard dreams

a moment ago an angel,
in the dark space of my delusion
with the softest touch of feathered wings
turned real into illusion,
gently relacing broken strings,
a tender kiss upon my cheek,
filling me with unknown peace,
though never did he speak

a moment ago an angel,
in a single heartbeat, less a tear,
appeared as though within a dream,
and softly drew me near
I arise, now strong and lean
and in wonderment I sigh,
for in blindness did I live my life
and with sight restored, I die

In Comfort as We Cry

and if in grief, so well acquainted
as touched upon a death we shared
in life, therefore, once unrelated,
now we find a friendship there
each alone with thoughts together
standing near the one we loved
each a rose to leave forever
to rest beside a marble dove
one moment in the weeping rain
fair solace from nature's doom
softly now to drown the pain
beside this earthly tomb
to join two hands in lonely grief
and walk slowly from his side
to sigh in bittersweet relief
in comfort as we cry

Gaia

the life of a woman
multiplied
and opened to the caress
of the gods
breasts rounded with the cream
of mother's milk
eyes closed in the first warm rays
of the Sun's powerful kiss
against soft brown lips
scarcely touched
with dewy moisture
thick thighs spread
to make space
for the burgeoning circle
of a growing womb
bathing in the glow
of morning light
as Eos opens the heavens
and Hyperion rises

somewhere between

somewhere between
the end and the beginning
primordial moments
undone, reborn
emotions thawing bodies of stone
hot and cold running confusion
chaos transitions
through solid rock and bone
normal moves to one side
skewed
distorted by its own image
and I am breathless when it is done
clenching my teeth
against ecstasy
unwanted

humanity rehung

with bold strokes of brilliant hues
across a barren page
cutting to the marrow
of hidden hope and rage
spilling forth in vast array
emotions raw and plain
dividing and untying
healing hurt with pain
tears to wash the brushes
the spatterings that fall
laughter to dry the moment
and touch the wounded wall
that crumbles now between us
a chisel to the stone
to shape a solid symbol
to cut deeply to the bone
song raised in voices strong
each in their native tongue
of victory hard fought and won
of humanity rehung

Ivory Tower

There is a mighty tower
within a forest green
inside it sits a little man
who thinks himself a king
Carved of the finest ivory
exquisite to behold
adorned with jewels and silver
and touched with purest gold
It sparkles in the starlight
and shines beneath the sun
but in its many chambers
there is room for only one

He peers down from jaded windows
to survey his domain
leans his fevered forehead now
against the window pane
looks out across the rolling hills
that seem forever green
and carefully considers
the world made from his dream
He dreamt of wealth and beauty
and power all his own
and now he has his money
and a palace is his home

But he's not quite what he thinks he is
and his tower's not so grand
for all his jewels and money
can't make him half a man
His hills are merely bumpy ground
his forest's made of grass
and he is only regal
within his looking glass
In his heart, the blood runs cold
and his soul has turned quite sour
and he is just a little man
in a tiny ivory tower

exposure

my soul is exposed in candlelight
softly caressing painted skin
the scent rises on the air
warmed by the kiss of dark red wine
staining my lips
moaning music mates mythically
with the night's own sighs
naked breasts glowing
in the orange low burn
breathing in rhythm
with the wind
unaccompanied pleasure
against fleshy thighs
pulling deeper sounds
from a place within me
no one else dares walk
thunder crashes, lightning flares
guttural acknowledgment of
perfect timing in breathless glory
exposing my soul in candlelight
for the rain to wash clean

Expectations

you expect things from me
the feminine and dainty
walk softly with tiny steps
talk gently with muted tones
wait patiently for Mr. Right to appear
to validate my existence
to complete me

to hell with your expectations
shriveled phallus dreams
wet with anticipation of power
to hell with dainty and waiting
my life will be no lamb
to sacrifice on the altar
of your self-worth

dream your phallic dreams
and touch yourself
make your manly proclamations
feeding your desires with delusions
of my complicity
while I dance
my personal rhythm
in circles around you

My Soul Hurts

I can think of no
other way
to describe it

the depth of it escapes me

I am only a receptacle
unconditional
undeniable
undermined

it sickens me, cripples me

I let it live
untouched by the hands
that could destroy
repair
control

my soul hurts

I hate, therefore I
might one day love
or perhaps
I have already

Hope

I long for hope tonight
a glimmer of light
against the gloom
 follow me down
 I'm falling
  for you
tunneling deeper
 can you see
 the light
it slides
against my skin
into the cracks
 is it time
 to wake up
  is it time
  to feel again
break open
rise up
like being born
full grown
ready
 wary
shedding skin
what once held me
 back
  down
pulling on hope
like a jacket

The Mirror

in the maddening chaos
of a wicked, walled-in world
where bigots rule the masses
their hate like flags unfurled
a generation's genocide
comes off without a hitch
as the hatred born of pain and doubt
climbs to a fevered pitch
building through the centuries
of prejudice and fear
growing in the decades
of trials and treasured tears
the madness swirls and eddies
like the ocean's tides and waves
feeding like a cancer
on the terror it creates

it seethes beneath the surface
just barely out of sight
waiting for the moment
it can slip into the light
a cold, black hand, like death itself
slinks slowly from the dark
to reach into the shaded spot
found at a nation's heart
as daylight dawns, the aftermath
finds a country on its knees
gazing into its history
bared for all the world to see
we sit in utter silence
star in shock at what we see
for the horror in that silence
is the mirror in front of me

YHWH

Oh now, father of my father's god
descendent of the Elohim,
child of Atum and brother to El
you, with no name, no shame, no pain
turn back your eyes
to the children of your land
to the bloody rivers
flowing through her sands
precious life, spilled
in nameless service
to ego
speak again of love
of the brotherhood of man
welcome home the Elohim,
Atum and El
in the brotherhood of gods
that the path be marked
before them
touch the hearts of your chosen
release them of their anger
their hatred, their bloodlust
reinvest their spirit
their dreams
their hearts
fulfill them
as once they fulfilled you

tonight, we burn

tonight, I burn
burn through
burn down
  burn out
follow me at your own peril
  love me
  on your own dime
I want to eat the world
and spit it back out
  the taste of it
  coats my tongue
bitterroot and honey
  like fear and passion
    mixed on a spoon
hypocrisy and corruption
chaos dressed in taffeta
  phobic ranting and fury
    shoved into human form
burn it down, love
like a marshmallow
on a stick
  bring the fire
  light me up
    tonight, we burn

The Nature of Madness

I could swear I just saw Elvis
having dinner with the Dane
they were speaking Shakespeare's language
exchanging soliloquies and monologues
over burgers and Blizzards
Hamlet raged
in sleep deprived lunacy
about Ophelia's lust and ghosts and graves
while Elvis mumbled
something to do with Priscilla's hair and Cadillacs
and no one even noticed
as Elvis dribbled chocolate sauce
on his white lapel
Hamlet's voice cracked
and they laughed together
each understanding
the nature of madness

From Here

it was harsh and cold, his failure
and I, unable to forgive him
for his frailty, could not speak, nor cry
my eyes cast down against it
against him, ceased to see him

his words, the begging, hoarse pleading
pathetic and horrid, echoed in my head
long after he had fallen silent
unable to end it, long past the tender moments
when leaving would have made sense
grateful for the silence, afraid of it as well
wondering wherever can we go from here

the darkness

darkness seeking purchase
finding places to lurk, to hide
to ooze and bleed through the skin
slithering smoke of obscenity
masked in pretense of morality
come in, come in
as if it were not already
deeply inside of us
filling up and flowing out
through our words
through our hands
infecting one another
passing the darkness
passing the fear
still believing
we are right

The Shaman's Lament

hidden in the wind of dragon's wings
the cold of winter reaches me in the Dream
Earth Mother lies barren and shivering
the serpent coiled and sleeping
on a bed of hard, black stone
unable to awaken
children play at war like games
with arrows made of steel and fire
the north winds howl meaningless words
through canyons built of glass
the song lost in its pain
the air whispers
buzzing around my head
daughters of the Moon sway slowly in grief
their children sleep in the shadows
unable to find the Dream
across the arid plains of the waking world
the drums lie broken in the shifting sands
the flutes have fallen silent
in deference to the wailing winds
the voices of the Ancient Ones are lost
but those chosen ears
which pick out the words in pieces
and those chosen eyes who see
this fearsome nature of man

Breathing Fire

Mother Earth is breathing fire upon a line of distant sky
kissing her fair child farewell as the shadows and shades draw nigh
The dark daughter now arises from her bed of lavender blooms
and stretches nimble fingers out across the room
She kisses her pale cousin as she passes in the hall
and dips a knee in homage when she hears her father's call

Mother Earth is breathing fire upon a line of distant dawn
kissing her dark child farewell as the curtains are all drawn
The fair daughter now arises from her dewy, rose draped bed
and smiles for the moment, though her mind might change again
She waves to her brighter cousin as they pass along the way
And waits to touch her father's hand, pausing there to pray

Mother Earth is breathing fire, her fury frightening the sky
her iron heart resounding the toll of a battle cry
She arises now herself from her bed of hardened clay
and holds her head in disbelief, anger, grief, dismay
She stands upon the ages where once the world was born
And cries into the ashes, forsaken and forlorn

calamity

it isn't safe tonight
this feeling inside me roils
  boils
fury and fear
desperation
  can you taste it
   on my skin?
it cuts deep
  deeper than that
   lean into it
it fills me until I cannot breathe
I cannot move
  trembling hands
   press against my sex
   hiding

fingers stained with purpose
drag against
the fabric of who we are
> *who we think we are*

it isn't safe
> *maybe it never was*

illusions torn
shattered and despised
> *and I can only stare*

disbelief
tears
> *my skin is wet*
> *blood*

it breaks us open
> *and oozes into the light*

Fat

I heard you say
I was fat
and the word was foul
in your mouth
> *I was six*
> *and didn't know yet*
> *how being fat*
> *was wrong*

I heard you say
I was gross
disgusting
fat
> *I was twelve*
> *my body changing*
> > *and I hated myself*

I heard you say
obese
like it was a dirty word
like it was worse than murder
I was sixteen
and instead of going to prom
I sat home and cried
alone
ashamed

I heard you say
the words
I heard the way
my name sounded
in your mouth
I was vile
a thing
fat
and you let me know
it was an unforgivable sin

Tired

I am tired
the weight of a hundred stones
that tried to hold me
of a thousand arrows
hurled and pounded home
the heavy burden of
unexploded landmines
inside me

I am tired
filled with gallons of
salty waters shed
from the eyes of mothers
of fathers and sisters and brothers
of people lost, and people found

I am tired
my ankles swell and weaken
my skin bruises
on the lies of lovers
on the truth of haters
my lip splits open
on the good intentions
of the willfully ignorant
dancing mindless of the carnage

I am tired
but the war
has only just begun
and my armor
has gone to rust
leaving me no choice
but to carry on

Broken

I fell down tonight
      tripping over myself
          trying to hide
you didn't notice
          or pretended not to
I tried to turn around
make it easy
no need to follow
    old rules
        but why should I be the one
        who keeps your heart
        from breaking
why am I the keeper
of your sanity
your safety
your peace of mind?
    my heart
          the pieces still rattle
        and I am still broken
        open

What Have We Done

the world feels like apocalypse tonight
as the sky grows dark
> *no moon*
> *no stars*
>> *just the taste of ash*
quiet doom hangs over
the horizon
as the fires rage
as our history burns
> *and the acid of our sin*
> *pours down*
> *the cheeks of our children*
what have we done?
how is this
our legacy
> *fear races pride*
the cradle broken
the grave undug
> *no one survives*
>> *no one*
>> *finds the bodies*
leave them for
the bugs

Apocolypse

here we are
at the end of the world
everything grinds down
the roads are still
the waters grower clearer
the air is cleaner
and all it takes
is the removal of man
from the face of the earth

Longing

I lit a candle on the altar tonight
two in the morning
and I can't sleep
the moon is dark
the stars
hide
the stillness burns
against my skin
  alone
  alone
I sent you away
  and away you went
when I wanted
to beg you
  stay
    stay
now, here I sit
awake
alone
  alone
and I can't even smell you
on my sheets
  can't feel you
    inside of me

I Will Roar

you tell me to quiet my mind
to be still
listen you say, listen to me
listen to him, listen to them
they know what is best for you
he knows what you need
you know what I want
and your words, his words, their words
fill the air, fill my head
there is no room to be still or
I will be crushed beneath them
all swirling around each other
contradictory, conspiratorial, confusing
so I move, dodge
I stumble and fall
and still the words come
chasing me, tripping me
racing ahead to ambush me
just as I come close to free
I open my mouth, and the voice is not mine
you talk over me, pushing me aside
but this is my life
and none of you know
anything about me
I will not be still, I will not be quiet
I will not speak, I will roar
and when you hear me
you will be the one who is still

The Shaman's Song

the quiet sings of patience
born of intrepid souls
stealing through the tempered wood
with hearts that beat in echo
of the hides which beat beside me

the sun's first rays kiss morning
with the sound of daylight's sighs
and scarce within a moment's breath
the mix of flute and spirit's melody
lofting high above the plain
of my solitary watch

the drums call out in greeting
and the feathers of the eagle
dance upon the upturned air
marking time to the beat
the soul might dance to hear
the sprite has come to play

the lark in fancy harmony
voice to company the flute
and owl, hooting ominous
against the points of melodious passion
counters the friction

the wind, not to be forgot
speaks forward loudly
with deep and guttural sounds
sweeping the tune away and back again

the buffalo tempt the morning air
with trumpet blast
and percussion pounding the plain

the sun in perfect roundness
slides behind the softness
of the gentle pattering of rain
and the fire crackles and hisses
craving my attention
beyond all else

the song carries forth
the flute and drums play
while I Dream the rest
calling my soul from Otherworlds
to sing the song

Radiant

the flames of my excess
lick at the bones of my failure
reminding me I am nothing
ash and regret
pounded down
inside the shell
of who I am
beaten bloody
bruised and crushed
under the weight
of yesterday
burn me clean
of the demons
so that when I rise up
I will shine
radiant and strong

love

two old friends
confidants
cohorts
married before color tv
he holds her hand
when they cross the street
or for no reason at all
she still wipes
the corner of his mouth
when they eat spaghetti
he picks her roses
and daffodils
she bakes him pecan pie
gnarled hands racked with age
knees debilitated by time
and service
backs twisted
hunching them forward
canes and walkers
hearing aids and false teeth
but their love needs no words
to be heard

I Have Sinned

I have sinned
　　　let me say this slowly
I have wanted him
　　　　　craved him
I have tasted the salt
　　　of his skin and tears
　　　　　　and sweat
I have heard his intimate
　　　thoughts, desires, needs
listened to his hushed
　　　　　and silent prayers
I know all of him
　　　his body, his mind
　　　　　his soul
the touch of his eyes on my skin
the music of his breath in my hair
the rhythmic insistence of his heart
　　　　　here then is my sin
he has never seen my hand
　　　touching his hidden places
he only feels the sweet sensation
　　　　　of my affection
in my obsession of him
　　　I have brought him to me
and yet I can not be his
　　　　　nor he mine
we are each alone in our sin
　　　and his sin is forever
　　　　　mine

intimate strangers

in a generation raised on
Barbie dolls and speed
we race from day to day alone
trading life for greed
we search hopelessly eternal
against some unseen clock
for the perfect answer, the final clue
our own piece of the rock
in the end we settle restlessly
burying our anger
and bring forth children, multiply
with our intimate stranger

For Cassie

if I could
>I would take away your pain
I would cover you
>in happiness
>>fill you up with joy
if I could
>I would whisper in your ear
how beautiful you are
>how my heart delights
>>to know you
if I could
>I would hold you
until you believe
>that the world is a better place
>>with you in it
if I could
>I would sing
all the words inside my heart
>so you would know
>>I love you

Slay the Monsters

It is the color of my skin tonight,
white,
sits too close,
    strangles me
it's the way I love tonight
the way I live
    privileged by nothing more
    than the manner of my birth
want to be free of the implication
guilt by association
    define me
it wasn't me
my hand washes clean
    the blood isn't mine
        isn't yours
it's just society
bleeding slowly
vile words and angry fists
sharp like daggers
    cutting me
        cutting you
you can not judge
you can not decide
    who lives
who dies broken and painted red
put down the weapons of your own destruction
you're killing yourself
    slay the monsters instead

numb

the cold
blisters my skin
flushes me
until I'm numb

excessive waste
extreme

souls lost

we spin
dizzy
with pain
fear

the air
sticks
thick and unclean

to bones
broken
and stained

bitter dregs

last night's whiskey
coats my tongue
regret rides the hard edge
of my teeth
      I fell deep this time
I taste yesterday
when I hold my breath
      I have no palate
      for today
smoke circles me
the smell of fire
burning with rage
      soaks me
      cloaks me
am I alive
if I can not feel?
I am nothing
but a hangover
      bitter dregs
      at the bottom
      of the bottle

an ordinary man

there was little to regard,
a life lived full and hard
an ordinary existence,
the thrills of which had long since
vanished with the hazy dreams
of yesterday's unfocused beams
and cooled beside the water's shore,
resting, weary of worldly wars
and yet, within the simple face,
I find a mystery there to trace
one of peace in times of hate,
and love and life beyond his fate
each wrinkle, each and every line,
spans across space and time
to touch me here, years away
on this wet and cold winter day,
and I find myself evaluating
everything I've been debating
to find they now seem rather small
within the simpler scheme of all
there was so much there to regard,
a life lived full and hard,
a face of gentle, graceful power,
I find I've stared for near an hour
and still so very much I see,
within that face and within me

October is Burning

October is burning at midnight,
the dark retreats before the blaze,
the smell of dry and fiery leaves,
and the hand of god is stayed.
The rains begin their cooling, gentle fall,
weeping autumn's joy upon the flame
and chill, the first shade of winter's coming
upon my back is laid.
Capped by billowing clouds of fading greys,
muffled softly in a feathery drift of snow,
in silence now before the glacial tide
and warmed by candle's glow,
I await within my forest fair
the advent of my princely dreams,
upon the flood of April's warming
and a regal, princely steed.
October is burning as I and he
ride away from the light of flames.
He holds me and I feel it deep within.
He speaks, and I am tamed.

dancing queen

he wears gold earrings and glitter
black nail polish, sloppy and bitter
six inch heels, with scars on his knees
from playground fights with bullies

perfect cat eyes, immaculate skin
dances with abandon, lost in his spin
silk and leather, feather and bone
forgetting for now the conflict at home

and when the night's over, he washes his face
before he leaves his one happy place
changes his clothes and puts on his disguise
the truth only seen hidden deep in his eyes

Just Another Friday Night

sirens scream
so close to home
    so far away
unreal
    like background noise
cops and robbers on the tv

bullets fly
slam into walls
into flesh
    cover your ears
    cover your eyes
bodies move
gyrate
bass beats
punctuated
    pop
        pop
            pop
chaos shatters
against the glass
and we hide
    under, behind
dial the phone
cower in fear
    hold your breath
    try not to be seen
it's just another
Friday night

3 haiku

bleeding blue and black
seeping into skin and bone
words bloom into place

careless words spill out
anger and fear and fury
masking dread and love

smoke drifts lazily
warmed air coaxes life from within
light spills across your face

an ode to my tattoo

wrought in the pain of artistry
forever on my skin
bold strokes of black ink
outlining an image
chosen from a wall
offered up in sacrifice
to the great gods
of my forefathers
a sign of my devotion
to my craft
the mark of braver beauty
indelible
wrought in the pain of artistry
forever on my skin

the end

I'm out of sorts, tonight
ragged, run down
scraping bottom
 let me lie here
  staring up at nothing
   the weight of your breath on my chest
follow me down, tonight
leave behind the expectation
the judgment, the fear
lay with me
  instead of on me
  inside me
 can you feel
  the quiet
   as we die
where no one sees
where no one knows
 hide here
  fall to pieces with me
   close your eyes
the sun will come
lift us
revive us
 our pieces mingled as one
  our skin dirty
the end
only brings us
back to the beginning

Dear reader,

We hope you enjoyed reading *Tonight*. Please take a moment to leave a review, even if it's a short one. Your opinion is important to us.

Discover more books by Natalie J. Case at
https://www.nextchapter.pub/authors/natalie-j-case

Want to know when one of our books is free or discounted? Join the newsletter at http://eepurl.com/bqqB3H

Best regards,
Natalie J. Case and the Next Chapter Team

About the Author

Natalie J Case is a poet, writer, photographer, and wanderer. Currently calling California home, she shares her life with two feline queens named for Goddesses. Telling stories since she was a child, Natalie developed a taste for poetry at an early age. She has a huge trove of really bad poetry she keeps hidden in the closet of her office, along with piles of novels she hasn't finished, and others she's barely begun, myriad short stories she tinkers with from time to time, and other bits of collected words that live on her computer and in hundreds of notebooks on her shelves.

A lifelong book nerd who first read Tolkien at nine years old, Natalie's reading taste varies from Science Fiction to Historical Fiction with stops along the way to include Fantasy and Space Opera, Paranormal Thrillers, and pretty much anything else that strikes her fancy. Certified Star Wars nerd. Marvel girl, with a semi-secret affection for a few DC superheroes. Advocate for the LGBTQ+ community and the homeless.

She has four novels published and available in several formats, and a new trilogy on the way.

https://nataliejcase.com
https://www.facebook.com/authornataliejcase
https://twitter.com/nataliejcase
https://www.instagram.com/nataliejcase

Also available from Author Natalie J Case

Forever

Born in the dark before time, Amara walks forever, in search of peace with who she is and how she came to be, with the human heart that draws her out and the relentless hunger that drives her. She is, in turn a killer and a lover, a monster and a healer, a sinner and a savior. "Forever is a long time, filled with lifeless moments and ridiculous truths. If we are lucky it is punctuated a time or two with wonderful people and incredible adventure."

Available at Amazon.com in hardback, paperback and Kindle

Through Shade and Shadow
In Gathering Shade
Where Shadows Fall

When a serial killer inadvertently reveals that Shades, once thought to be nothing more than myth, do indeed exist, no one expected it to lead to a second civil war, or for an evil man to exploit the conflict to seize power. The war brings together Shades and Shadows, Shifters and Sages to fight for their lives, and try to save the country before it gets swallowed up in violence and bloodshed.

Available at Amazon.com in hardback, paperback and Kindle

Tonight
ISBN: 978-4-86750-706-3

Published by
Next Chapter
1-60-20 Minami-Otsuka
170-0005 Toshima-Ku, Tokyo
+818035793528
24th June 2021

CPSIA information can be obtained
at www.ICGtesting.com
Printed in the USA
LVHW090810140721
692545LV00004B/34

9 784867 507063